The Life
of
Johnston

Diary

2012

To

Enzo

January 12

Dear Max

A few days ago Teresa and I were watching *Parenthood* on TV. A doctor told the parents that their son had Asperger's syndrome. They had their dramatic, tearful TV reaction. Teresa said, "Do you think that's what we'd do if someone told us Enzo was ugly?"

We both think he's freakishly beautiful. One of Teresa's friends told her he has a six-pack, and we've been repeating it to each other ever since. It's not a garish six-pack. It's just that he has this wonderful strong animal body. After his bath the other day he was standing naked at the kitchen sink running water through a snorkel to see it shoot up the other end, absorbed and busy. And I was checking out his butt. It has those wonderful dished-in sides. And it occurred to me that someday I might not be allowed to do that anymore.

January 20

Dear Max,

Yesterday in the middle of trial I had such a bad coughing fit that I had to leave the courtroom. The trial went on without me. (That's how important I am.) A guy in the hallway tried to help me by getting some water and hovering with it. I recovered, but as I did, he started to not be able to get his breath. He backed away from me, bending over, heaving and crying.

I followed him, clucking with concern. After a few minutes he got better, and we started to talk. Turns out he is Detective Daniels, under subpoena to testify in our case. "But I can't remember anything," he said. He explained that he'd been run over and dragged under a car, and now he can't remember things that happened before that. (Our case is four years old.) "I'm just afraid I'll be up there in front of everyone and I won't remember." I remembered reading about that in the paper. It was a big attempted murder case. He was on duty, trying to make an arrest, and the guy decided to run him over.

I tried to think of every comforting thing to say. Like every witness in this case has said they don't remember stuff because it was four years ago. And if anyone has a good reason to not remember, it's him. "You're a hero," I said.

We talked about our kids, and his head injury. He showed me pictures from his surgery. He told me about his wife who died of cancer and his wife now who is leaving him because of his problems.

A coughing fit is nothing compared to post traumatic stress, but there was something about how we had both been out of control that made this quick, temporary friendship possible. We were jolted out of our roles and into humanity.

He ended up not testifying that day. He was ordered back for Monday—so this whole weekend, there'll be dread.

Afterward I had these fantasies about how he would testify and he would look over at me and I would look at him and give him Courage and everyone would somehow see this, and I would look like Ms. Florence Nightingale Defense Attorney.

There's so much vanity mixed up with our compassion—or at least mine. To me, that doesn't cheapen it.

*

Enzo still has some proportions of a baby, or at least a toddler. His head is about twice as big as his but.

February 8

Dear Max,

I just settled down to write in my diary for the first time in weeks. It's almost five thirty. Enzo will wake up around six or six thirty. And Duncan just took this gurgling shit in his cat box. He's covering...the smell just hit me. Must get up and clean cat box. No wonder fame continues to elude me.

Back now. All I have are notes I've made over the last few weeks:

Enzo announced, "No one knows what my life is like."

I didn't write down the context for this announcement, but I think it was me asking him to do some normal task—put on his shoes perhaps, and this was his protest.

Another time he was in the bath, and I was using my wet hands to sort of fluff his hair and get it a little wet, not even really washing it because he really doesn't like that, and he yelled, "Stop it! Are you trying to destroy me?"

He also likes to say, by way of general protest, "Are you saying I'm not even your *son*?"

*

Our family is obsessed with butts. Teresa has explained to Enzo that my butt is the biggest butt in the family, then hers, then his, then Duncan's and then the fish. So Enzo announced to me: "You have the best butt in the family. And the biggest. And the deadliest."

*

"I drink juice so I can be famous."

*

"That makes, like, no sense!" (He's a Valley Girl now. Actually he learned that from Shaggy on *Scooby Doo*.)

*

We have Enzo's friends over for movie night sometimes. We rearrange all the furniture in the living room and project the movie up on a wall, so it's really big and like a real movie. One of Enzo's friend's moms thought *Scooby Doo* might be a little too scary, but she left her kid anyway. Her kid was fine, by the way.

Later she told me that her family had watched *Mary Poppins* and the kids just loved it and they were thinking about having some kids over to watch *The Sound of Music*. I told Teresa, and she said, "The only way Enzo would watch *The Sound of Music* is if the Nazis blew up Maria."

Enzo did end up going over there for movie night. They watched *Ice Age*.

*

We got a wedding invitation. It had three pictures of the couple, and the caption said, "A Love Affair, Something Special in the Air," and Teresa added, "From my derriere."

I wonder if people are a little abashed about getting married when we can't. Probably not. They're deep in their own problems. Like having a wedding, which sounds like complete hell to me.

February 12

Dear Max,

Teresa got lobster tails at Safeway. They were five dollars each on sale. Last night Enzo went over to Ben's for movie night. When Teresa dropped him off, Ben's parents asked what we were doing? Going out to dinner? A movie perhaps? Teresa didn't want to say that we were just staying home and watching TV and eating pizza, so she said, "We decided to stay home for a nice grown up dinner." They asked what we were having and Teresa said, "Lobster tails."

"It just came out," she said when she told me about it. "I mean the kids were going to be having pizza and watching TV, and it just sounded lame. So anyway, when you go pick him up, if anyone asks you how the lobster tails were, just say they were great."

I adore this kind of small conspiracy. It's a tiny piece of us-against-the-world. Lobster tails! Hurrah!

February 16

Dear Max,

I'm at work but I've decided to go on strike and just read and write and eat. Maybe go for a bike ride. Maybe go to the movies. I feel inspired.

I got jolted out of my routine a little bit because I left my bike at work last night so I had to take the light rail to work today. I was sitting at the light rail station feeling the warmth from the rising sun on my eyelids and thinking about how I used to write in the morning and that maybe we should go camping in Death Valley and wake up and feel the sun on our faces in the cold morning and hear the silence, and then I thought maybe I should get a tent for the back yard and it would be my writing tent—my own little office—and I would furnish it with rugs and a fabulous recliner and of course a desk and bookshelves. And then I would be a writer again.

I used to go around with this marvelous inner alertness. Anything that happened might be something to write about. Fuck-ups and misfortunes were especially rich sources of material. I felt like an outsider, off balance and a little scared and a little bold.

Now I sort of know what I'm supposed to be doing, and a lot of the time I feel like I can do it. I have a place in the world. I think about work and money and food and how fat I'm getting. And I think about Enzo and Teresa. They're still interesting, thank goodness, and, like the best people in books, always themselves and always surprising.

I'm reading *The Life of Johnson* again, and this time I keep getting this wonderful feeling of warmth and affection between these unbelievably lovable men. Even the *ands* and *buts* are full of love.

March 3

Dear Max,

I slept in until 6:30, and *so did everybody else.* I don't know what to do with myself. I feel as though I've been to a spa.

Back in preschool, Enzo used to talk about girls and play with them at school, and even worship a few of them—remember Casey? And now he doesn't. In kindergarten the boys hang out together and the girls hang out together. In preschool it was the same way, except Enzo hung out with both. Teresa used to tell me about all the girls, and Enzo, in the top of the play structure, eating their lunches together. The only girl he talks about now is Peyton, one of his friend's little sisters, because she can run so fast and wrestle even though she's only three.

I'm sure soon I'll be hearing that boys go to Mars to get more candy bars while girls go to Jupiter to get more stupider. (When I was young it was the other way around, at least in my circle.)

He's learning insults that we don't think we taught him. At dinner, he said that Schuyler is, like, a crazy geek. (But it wasn't crazy, it was something stranger that I can't remember now.) We told him not to call names and to be nice to other kids, especially if they don't have many friends. Later Teresa told me Schuyler *is* a crazy geek.

Enzo wears holes in the left knee of every pair of pants in a matter of days. Apparently that's his landing knee. Then I patch them, and he wears holes in the patches.

March 7

Dear Max,

I am foiled. Foiled.

I decided to reclaim my writing life. I bought coffee. (I blame tea and Enzo for my decline.) I set my alarm for five thirty, opened my diary on my computer, and put the computer on the coffee table in front of the couch.

This morning the alarm went off in the middle of a dream that had something to do with being newly married to this nice rich old man. It was friendly and surprising. Teresa curved around me, warm and soft. "Duncan got me up at four, and it's my day off." (Meaning her day off from the gym.) After a while we got up. For some reason she made a race out of it, climbing over me to get up first. When I did get up, she pulled my pajama pants down and was gone.

I lit the gas fire and some candles, made a latte, just like in the old days, sat down and got comfortable on the couch...

"Maamaaaa! Mama-Kate! Mama-Kate!"

Maybe he sensed that I had nothing to write about. I lay down with him for a while and tried to convince him to go back to sleep. No go. I got up and told him to go back to sleep by himself. Yeah right. In about three minutes he was up, announcing cheerfully. "I'm awake!"

Luckily, yesterday Teresa got him these cool sticky string things that you twist into shapes, and he's playing those as I write. "Hey look Mama-Kate!" He shows me a styracosaurus hanging off the edge of the coffee table with a sticky string wrapped around its tail and the other end stuck onto a Kleenex box, which is somehow holding the whole thing up.

He keeps farting, loud and clap-like, to our mutual satisfaction. And he just rolled up a sticky string into a ball and stuck it in my ear.

March 8

Dear Max,

Enzo's into this lurid *National Geographic* series called *Nature's Deadliest*. It's about predators and various sorts of poisonous creatures. His favorite parts are the reenactments of when people get bitten or eaten. For the African Rock Python—a snake he already adored— they showed a pretend X-ray to demonstrate how the snake unhinged its jaws and expanded its ribs to make room for a creature bigger than itself. Then for a touch of realism they showed the giant snake all swollen with having just eaten something and two human feet (fake I hope) wiggling out of its mouth.

Enzo was entranced. We keep telling him it's not real and not to be scared and he keeps insisting that it is real, and he obviously likes it that way. He's not scared at all, and he's absolutely on the side of the eater, not the eatee.

*

Right now our favorite thing to do is he sits on my butt while I pretend to be asleep. I snore loudly and then let fly a series of explosive farts, lifting my butt off the bed higher each time as the farts get louder until he falls off. Teresa started it. One morning she said to Enzo, "Want to know what I listen to all night long?" Then she started snoring loudly and making loud, long fart noises. And now every night at dinner he says, "What do you hear at night, Mama-Teresa?" And she does it again. Then she does Enzo (quieter farts and softer snores) and then Duncan (little farts and loud meows) and then herself (dignified silence).

March 9

Dear Max,

Left to his own devices, Enzo usually doesn't zip his pants. Or wipe his ass, come to think of it. I taught him the expression, "XYZPDQ!" which stands for, "Examine Your Zipper Pretty Darn Quick!" But even when he examines it, he doesn't zip it.

Last night at dinner he announced, "GSEPY!" and looked at us expectantly.

"What does that stand for?" I said.

You could see him thinking or a second. "Make popsicle sticks!"

As Enzo would say, that makes, like, *no sense.*

*

Here are some notes from the last few weeks, in no particular order:

Enzo, going on and on about his penis surgery, asking me to tell the story again, and then telling parts of it himself. And then he adds in a whisper, "But it's not very good to talk about. *It's private.*"

*

Enzo, resisting me as I try to put lotion his itchy arms: "I think my arms are out of business for today."

*

This note says, "Up my butt Charles Dickens." The whole family is into this improvisational rhyme routine. (I think it's from an old Eddie Murphy sketch.) For example, "Gonna do a little dance, up my butt! Have a fine romance, up my butt!" Or, "Got a little blender up my butt! It's really tender up my butt!" One person starts it, and then everyone tries to come up with a rhyme. So Enzo threw out, "Got some chickens up my butt!" We all looked at each other, stumped, Enzo delighted to have stumped us, completely satisfied with just the chickens, and then Teresa got a light in her eye and came in with, "Got Charles Dickens up my butt!" I came in right behind with, "It's real slim pickins up my butt!"

*

Enzo accidentally sat down hard on this inch-long hard plastic pylon that's probably part of some Lego set. He got up and craned his neck around to look at his butt, then held it with both hands. "Mama-Kate, I think my butt is kind of damaged."

March 10

Dear Max,

It's Saturday morning. Enzo woke up at 5:30 again. I got in bed with him and tried to snuggle him back down. It didn't take. He kept saying he needed to get up, and I kept saying it was too early, and finally I said he could get up and play but I wasn't ready to get up and read to him. He crawled over me and out of bed. "I have to go pee so bad, and I'm scared." (The hallway was dark.) I got up, and he walked down the hall ahead of me saying, "Now you're up!"

He peed into the plastic pee receptacle left over from his surgery. "Mama-Kate, look! It's, like, 900 gallons!"

I held it up to the light, reading the measurements on the container. "Wow. Five hundred milliliters."

Five hundred!"

"Shhhh! Mama-Teresa's still asleep."

He walked down the hall, stood outside our bedroom door and stage-whispered to Duncan and Teresa, "Guys! It was five hundred!"

*

Now he's playing by himself, and I'm writing. It's wonderful that he doesn't want my attention every moment anymore. A few weeks ago he was playing in his room, and I went in there to check on him, and he said, "Stop bothering me," and shut the door, and I was like, *YES!*

March 11

Dear Max,

Six-thirty, and Enzo's awake, playing out here in the living room with a shark, a super hero that I can't identify, and an allosaurus. Since I seem to be stuck with him, I'm going to try to transcribe his play.

*

Up go shark. Sorry it was a crash. Wssshhhhhh Wssshhhhh (deep scratchy voice) *Up from the depths. Have to get some submarines, slam jaws! Whoa, he's biting our car, he must be humungous...stuck in...cracker...zzp-zzp-zzp...who are you? I am Enzo, defender of the earth, ka-pow.* (Now he's making the shark bite down on one of his sticky string toys.) *Put that on my tail. I'll do it for...let's go, go, go, go* (whispering) *Holy cow. Ka-boom, whoa...up from red depths, who are these stars? Enzo!* (Now he's face to face with the shark, roaring at it.)

I can't understand a lot of what he says, and I have to leave that part out. But aside from that, I think a lot of the story is vivid inside his head, continuous and whole, but unspoken.

March 12

Dear Max,

I dreamed about you last night, Max. I remember almost none of it. There was some scandal and a tent with a table in it and desserts. You said you didn't like going to town just to get groceries because it always turned out to be more than that.

But that doesn't give the feeling of the dream at all.

*

Duncan is sitting beside me looking inquiringly at my lap, which is occupied by my computer. The time changed last night, so now five-thirty, when my alarm goes off, is really four-thirty. It's six now. Which is really five. At least Enzo isn't up.

*

Enzo and I have been swimming every day for the last three days. I said that we're amphibians. "Mama-Teresa's a reptile," he said—a gorgeous compliment coming from him.

*

He amuses himself in the water now, and I can swim a lap and then come back and check on him. He has goggles and a nose clip and loves swimming under water, practicing his death roll and just hanging out down there. He used to swim in the deep end all the time, but lately he hasn't. I asked him about it, and he said, "Ever since I got my underwater skills—my underwater abilities—I don't go in the deep end any more." I guess now that he can see how deep it is, it seems scary. Before, when he couldn't touch the bottom in any part of the pool or see how deep it was, the whole pool was deep, and I was always right there with him.

March 13

Dear Max,

Last night I washed Enzo's hair. He hates that, and I hardly ever do it. He hollered and thrashed about, but it was over pretty fast and then he lay back in the water rinsing his hair by swishing it around. I held up a towel for him to dry his hair so the water wouldn't run into his eyes. It was all over. But he still kept yelling, "Stop it! Stop it! Stop it!"

"It's all over," I said.

"Stop it! Stop it!"

I walked away and started picking up the house, and he kept on and on. Finally I went back in there and sat down by the tub and just looked at him. He was crying and still really mad.

"You're not even my mother—I'll not have any parents—I'll not have any friends—I'm moving away—call the workmen—I'm canceling school—I'll not be friends with Keelan, or Ben, or even Isaac!"

Teresa came in from the egg (her studio) and said, "What's going on in here? I can hear you from outside." I explained. "Well it's all over now." By this time Enzo was wrapped in a warm towel and sitting on my lap on the couch. (We put his towel and pajamas in the drier while he's in the bath, so you see how he suffers.) Snot was smeared on his otherwise clean face. He was starting to calm down. "I'll go get your nice warm pajamas," said Teresa. She got them, and he put them on with this air of resignation. Then I read to him for an hour and he went to bed.

*

A few days ago, Teresa told me, "Enzo farted while I was wiping his butt." Then she looked at him accusingly, "Twice!" He glowed.

*

Enzo said, "When Mrs. Korte says to do something, I obey! She always sabotages me. And then she says, 'Oh my! Ooooh my!'"

"What does sabotage mean?" I said.

"It's when you say, 'Look up, look down, look up, look down.'"

"Let's look it up in the dictionary." I skipped over the complicated part about hostile agents and just read the end: "'To destroy or render useless.' Does that sound right?"

"Yeah. *Destroy.*"

*

A few weeks ago I was talking with some parents who were choosing which schools to try for in the public school lottery. They wanted to know why we chose the public Waldorf for Enzo.

"Well, he really isn't into letters and numbers, and Waldorf isn't either—not in the first couple of years."

"Oh, so is he more into art and music?"

"No, not really."

"Oh."

"He's more into weapons."

March 14

Dear Max,

Last night when Enzo got out of his bath, I wrapped the warm towel around him, and he said something that I wanted to remember. I repeated it aloud to fix it in my mind until I could scribble it down. And then I forgot to scribble it down, and now it is gone, gone, gone.

You have to write down what he says right away or it's gone. I can remember his habitual expressions. Like he says, "I'll not" instead of "I won't." But fresh subjects have to be caught fresh.

All this is leading up to why I have nothing to write about today.

Yesterday Teresa and Enzo got home almost forty-five minutes late. They were at the Children's Museum, which is about ten miles away on the freeway. It was raining, and surely the traffic was bad. And Teresa wouldn't call when she was driving, especially in the rain. Finally I called her and left a message that said, "Don't pick this up if you're driving, but where are you?" Of course she didn't pick up because she was driving.

Anyway, I started to think about the two car seats—one is rated safer than the other—and hope that Teresa put Ben, Enzo's friend, in the less safe one. And I planned what I would say to Teresa's mom when she wanted to give Teresa a Catholic funeral. I wouldn't allow it. I wondered how I would get to the hospital if they were hurt. We only have one car, and in the fantasy, they had just totaled it. I'd ride my bike. Or call Karol.

And the whole time I enjoyed being alone and cooking dinner and having some wine and listening to the news on the radio. And then they got home, safe and alive, and we all walked to the corner store together to get jellybeans.

March 15

Dear Max,

"Mama-Kate, you have some blue on your elbow."

"I wonder what that is."

"Cancer!"

"How did you learn about cancer?"

"I was watching a grown-up show with Mama-Teresa."

March 16

Dear Max,

Yesterday as I was leaving for work, Enzo wanted me to help him make a robot. He had some pennies and a piece of Kleenex as raw materials and was asking for popsicle sticks.

"How do you make a robot?" I said.

"I'm just thinking. In my mind. You feed him coins."

*

Last night we were reading his sex ed book about boy parts and girl parts and where babies come from. "I want to study it." He made me get up, and we both dug through his toy basket until we found a magnifying glass. Then he studied the pictures with it. When it was time for bed, he pulled down his pajama bottoms and announced, "I'm studying my penis," peering at it through the magnifying glass.

*

Two nights ago at dinner, I made tiny baby potatoes tossed in olive oil and salt. Of course Enzo didn't want them, and we had to force him to take just one bite, or he wouldn't get any jellybeans, and his one bite was this tiny crumb-sized morsel, which he dramatically spit out, protesting that he didn't like it. The next morning while we were reading books, he farted and then had the gall to say, "I think it was a potato fart."

This is why, whenever we talk about him when he's not around, we refer to him as, "Your ingrate son."

March 19

Dear Max,

Last night as he was going to bed Enzo announced, "I'm popular."

"Why do you say that?"

"The kids in Fourth R all like me. Even the six-year-olds. And even seven-year-olds." (Fourth R is an afterschool daycare that he goes to once a week. Six and seven-year-olds are elementary school aristocracy as far as he's concerned.)

"How did you learn what popular means?"

"I think it was Obama."

Teresa and I weren't popular. She was an art-geek and an outcast. I didn't have any friends that I liked, and the friends I had weren't cool anyway. We disdained the popular people, in my case because that was the only option. And I still think there's something about being popular in high school that doesn't bode well for the future. It's occurring to me only this moment that even popular people can end up with friends they don't like. But we both desperately want Enzo to be popular.

This weekend Enzo went to a girl's birthday party. All the girls from class were invited and two boys, and Enzo was one of the two, to our delight. I don't think the other boys like girls as much as he does. He told me he's going to marry Kylie and Collette. I told him he can only marry one, and he explained that he's going to have babies with both of them.

I have some notes here:

"My butt is so flexible I can stick out one butt cheek."

*

"I don't like food." (I don't think we're actually related.)

*

Max, I just want you to know that while I've been writing this I've gotten up twice to persuade Enzo to go back to sleep (didn't take). I've also helped him measure his dragon fly (6.5 inches), had several conversations about where he might find Green Lantern, and set up his easel and paints for water colors. And now he's calling out, "Mama! Where are my scissors?" It's a fucking miracle I write anything at all. It's six thirty, for the record, and Enzo just called out, "Mama, did you hear me fart?"

March 20

Dear Max,

It's five-thirty. Dark out. I have coffee. Duncan is shitting.

There's something I wanted to write about. I was thinking about it last night, and it was almost written in my mind, and now I don't know what it is. Maybe cleaning the cat box will clear my head.

I remembered. (It worked!) Miss Lish, the movement teacher at Enzo's school, died. We got a call from the school and an email. "We just have to remember, he has no empathy," said Teresa. Like in one of his crocodile books they show the contents of a crocodile's stomach, which includes a human head and an arm. And he's totally thrilled.

But Miss Lish was young and pretty and lively, and he saw her every Tuesday. Today is Tuesday. She taught something called eurhythmy, which is a dance and movement technique that's part of the Waldorf curriculum.

These days when someone young dies I get this dread around my heart. I invent reasons that whatever happened to them could never happen to Enzo. I view their parents with superstitious horror and distaste. Like this one DA's daughter fell off a horribly high bridge where she was drinking with friends and died.And when I saw the mom in court, I thought, *She had four kids, and I only have one, so that could never happen to me.*

Or another lawyer, a rich private defense attorney, was sitting downstairs in the jail waiting to see a client. I was there too, talking with one of the public defenders.

Our kids—how old now?—grow up so fast!—school already—were just babies—always babies to us. And then I remembered that the rich lawyer's sixteen-year-old son had recently slammed his new Mustang into a tree and died. *Shut up, shut up, shut up*, I thought. But also, *That could never happen to Enzo because all he'll be driving when he's sixteen is a twenty-year-old Ford Focus.*

Mrs. Korte told the kids about Miss Lish, and Enzo didn't say much about it to us. He doesn't seem to mind. Mrs. Korte assures us that this is very age-appropriate.

March 26

Dear Max,

We all went to Vegas. I had a forensics conference, and Teresa and Enzo came along. Before we left, Teresa told Enzo to go to the bathroom because the toilet on the plane was really small. Enzo said, "That's okay, so's my butt."

I also have a note here: "You guys should sell my butt to a museum and people could look at it." It's tempting. He *is* a first class pain in the ass, and we need the money.

The conference was what they always are: you could learn the same thing from a book in a quarter the time. But we had a great time in our fabulous hotel room, thirty-second floor with a view of the airport, maybe not a plus for everyone, but for us, perfect.

One picture I'd like to keep in my mind is Teresa sitting at that huge wall-size window, still and intent, a dark outline against the night sky, watching the planes take off and land. She said she found it soothing.

The hotel was super fancy. It had a wave pool and an endless river (a pool with a current that goes round and round) and a regular pool and a Jacuzzi. Enzo was submerged about five hours each day, and now he has a tan line on his face from his swimming mask. He also got to watch TV to his heart's content.

It was three days in a completely artificial environment—and completely satisfying.

April 2

Dear Max,

It's ten after five, and I'm tired and pissed. Enzo kept waking up last night and calling for me. Between 12 and 1:30 I think he did it three times. After each time I'd finally be back in bed, almost asleep and then, "Mama Kate!...Mama Kate!" The only reason I'm up now is he did it again at 4:55.

Time to write about how god damn cute he is.

Yesterday afternoon we were at the park. A girl, maybe thirteen or fourteen, arrived, walking on crutches. Her leg was in a big, old-fashioned cast (not that boot that you sometimes see). Enzo kept checking her out, playing close to where she was sitting. After a while he said, "Can we tell that girl about my penis surgery?" But by then she was getting ready to go, and I explained that that might be awkward anyway.

"What does awkward mean?"

"It means she might wonder why we're telling her about your penis. It might seem strange because we don't know her."

She left, and Enzo walked out to the sidewalk two or three times to watch her slow progress down the street.

"Sometimes I like grownup girls in casts," he said.

A few minutes later, "Do you think we could phone call her?"

"We don't know her phone number. Or her name."

"But does your phone have a picture of people and then you call them?" I explained that it does, but only for people we know whose number I actually put into the phone.

And a few minutes later he said, "I think about girls in casts all the time. I still like snakes though." And then a turtle that someone brought to the park turned our attention.

Later that night as he was going to sleep Enzo called me into the bedroom. "I have to tell you a secret."

I leaned down and he whispered in my ear, "I like broken-leg girls. It's so interesting."

*

Some notes from the past week, unrelated and in no particular order:

"Sometimes when I get cold, I get freaked out."

*

"I have a strange feeling. As strange as twenty aliens."

*

"Can you write in your diary—my farts are loud."

*

"Somehow my butt feels strange."

April 9

Dear Max,

Enzo and I just got back from a trip to Annie and Todd's. I have to get ready for work now, but the one thing I want to make sure I remember is when we got off the train, Teresa and Enzo walking in front of me, talking so eagerly, his little body all excited to see her, looking up at her, telling her the news, and Teresa holding his hand, leaning down to listen in the noise of the train station.

The night before I had been lying with Enzo in bed and I said that I'd miss Annie and Todd and Emmet, but I'd be happy to get home to Teresa. I asked if he missed mama Teresa. He said no. Then he started crying a little. It wasn't fake crying, exactly. There were real tears, real sadness. But he seemed conscious of being a tragic figure. (I'm familiar with this sincere but self-dramatizing state of mind. In fact I live in it.) And then he said, "Mama Teresa is better than Annie and Todd and Emmet."

When we got home I told Teresa what he'd said, and she said, "*Really?*" I have to admit, it doesn't sound like him.

I also want to put down here the picture of my dad and Enzo racing down the beach on the flat wet sand, my dad in rolled up jeans, Enzo in his blue shorty wetsuit, splashing in the white water, face alight.

By the way we're absolutely mad about the wetsuit. It's so becoming.

April 10

Dear Max,

I'm embarrassed to record here that, once again, we are on a campaign to make Enzo sleep through the night without calling me in there three, four, sometimes five times. I was reading last year's diary around this time, and it said exactly the same thing. We are backsliders.

At Annie and Todd's he only got me up once. I asked him why that was. He didn't know. I asked if it was because I was right there on the floor beside him, and he said yes. Then we had our first night back at home, and he got me up four times. Fuck. The worst is when I'm almost back to sleep and I hear his little voice again, "Mama Kate!"

I asked if he had any ideas about how to just get me up once a night the way he used to. He didn't. I told him to think about it and I would too, and we'd talk again when I got home from work. At dinner I asked if he'd had any ideas. He hadn't. But then he said something that Teresa and I didn't understand, but it had something to do with the first night and the second night. "Try it again after you swallow that bite," said Teresa. He chewed and swallowed.

"So on the first night...?" I said.

"On the first night I call you two times."

"Okay. And on the second night...?"

"On the second night I call you one time. Deal?"

Teresa and I looked at each other and she nodded.

"Deal," I said, "And guess what else? If you only get me up two times tonight, I'll get you a donut hole from Marie's."

"What about a toy?"

"A donut hole is good. And the first time you call me zero times, I'll get you a whole donut."

And right now, I am ecstatic to report, it is six in the morning and he only got me up two times. This sleeping in till six is just icing on the cake.

April 11

Dear Max,

Enzo lost his first tooth yesterday. It had been loose for a while, and when he bit into his sandwich at dinner, it hurt. It was hanging by a thread. He rocked it and rocked it, and out it came to the intense delight of the whole family. Enzo handed the bloody, spitty thing to me, and Teresa said, "Wash it off so we can see it. Wait, I'll do it," taking charge of the family treasure. She washed it and we all gazed at it. Enzo inquired about the tooth fairy, and we reviewed the procedure. He asked where the tooth fairy lives. I said since Santa lives in the North Pole, maybe the tooth fairy lives in Antarctica. He looked skeptical and said that actually she lives in the Indian Ocean. He also said, "I feel like a grown up kid now."

So last night he was waiting for the Tooth Fairy and also trying to call me into his bedroom only one time. He woke up around midnight crying and crying and said he didn't want to do it—it was too hard. I finally got him back to sleep. He woke up one more time around four in the morning and called out "Mama Kate!" We waited, silent, hoping he'd fall back asleep. Then he said in this mournful sleepy voice that his tooth was gone but there was no present. Fuck. The tooth must have gotten lost in the crying episode, which also involved a lot of rearranging of blankets and pillows. But then—miracle—he fell asleep again without us going in there, and Teresa slipped his present under his pillow, a book of games and puzzles.

April 12

Dear Max,

A few days ago I heard Enzo telling Teresa, "I have an adaptation to survive Mama Kate's farts." She asked him what that was and he said, "I bite her on the butt."

April 23

Dear Max,

I've been working on my 1994 diary, getting it ready to publish on Kindle. The copy on my computer is one I edited for publication about 16 years ago, when that one publisher said she might take it if I made it more like a book. It's amazing how anticipating someone else's taste just screws you up. The edits are terrible. The additions are shameful, and—I blush to say—some are fictionalized. Luckily I have a paper copy of the original, so I'm restoring the copy on my computer to its original form. It takes fucking forever.

This is all by way of explaining why I haven't written in this present diary in over a week.

*

We just got back from a weekend at Lake Tahoe. Enzo met a girl at the beach with a *cast*. He loves girls with casts. We were all climbing on some big boulders in the lake. They're attached to the land but mostly surrounded by water. Kyriana kept asking me for help getting up to the bigger rocks, and I kept saying no because I didn't want her to end up somewhere she couldn't get down from by herself. Then she lost her grip and slid a little way down a boulder into the water. She was crying and yelling for help. Her brother and I pulled her out, while Enzo looked on, entranced.

Enzo has made me tell that story about five times in the last twelve hours. Teresa took a picture of the two of them standing on the beach, and he keeps insisting on looking at on her camera. And when Kyriana left he chased down the trail after her to say goodbye. Teresa went with him and she reported that he hugged her. Then he wanted to go back to those boulders and have me point out the exact spot where she slipped into the water.

When we first met her, Enzo was too shy to talk to her, but he desperately wanted to discuss her medical history and his own. He kept standing off by himself, close to her, but not really with her, staring out at Lake Tahoe and saying, "My testicle was up here, but then I had surgery, and now it's down here. I had a cast on my penis, and I couldn't even move. But that's not good to talk about. It's private."

But then they just started playing, and she talked a blue streak, and he listened and listened and listened. At one point the two of them were standing on the beach, facing each other, showing how they could whistle, both of them just barely able to do it, but still doing it, pleased with themselves and each other.

*

I just read a sort of diary/essay by one of my friend Caroline's students, and it made me so jealous I can't see straight. It also made me feel like writing, not working. Yay! (I'm at work, and I never write at work.)

Anyway, it was just full of people, and so smart and funny. It made me think that young people are maybe just better. (Obviously this is an unusual young person, but still.)

My mind has been going for a while now. I'm not just talking about that settling down to ready-made thoughts so that you don't have to think about anything that seems to happen to almost everyone eventually. I'm talking about actual mental deterioration. Like a few weeks ago I tried to put the garbage can in the fridge, and the only reason I didn't do it is that it wouldn't fit. Not that I stood there trying to cram it in. I just opened the fridge and then paused, garbage can in hand, thinking, *something is not right*. And then I figured it out.

And I use the wrong words. Like yesterday a ladybug landed on my arm and I said to Enzo, "Look! A butterfly!"

"What?!"

"I mean..." (trying to think of the word).

"*Lady*bug!"

May 4

Dear Max,

We take turns thinking of impossible things. Such as, Duncan (the cat) wearing sunglasses and snowboarding while chewing gum. And we try to top each other. So Teresa came up with, Mama-Kate in skinny jeans. That's it. Well, it was a winner. I think the game broke up after that because this could obviously never be topped. And ever since, Enzo's been saying to me, at random times, "Mama-Kate in skinny jeans!" And then he totally cracks up. Teresa said I should blow his mind and actually *get* some skinny jeans.

*

On a similar theme, Enzo told me, admiringly, that I have the biggest butt in the whole human race.

*

Enzo knows all about the Triassic, Jurassic and Cretatous eras, all the way down to the age of mammals—that is the present. He refers to the time when Teresa and I were children simply as The Ancient. As in, "Did you guys just read books in The Ancient?"

*

I told Enzo that back when I was a little girl we lived in the country, and we couldn't just walk to the corner store to get candy, so sometimes Annie and her friend Jennifer would ride Jennifer's pony, Strawberry, all the way to Los Olivos—three miles each way—to buy candy. And then I told him all the candy I could remember from my childhood, especially the gum: Bubble Yum, Bubblicious, and best of all, Hubba Bubba. He listened with rapt attention. And later, lying in bed, he said, "Mama Kate, tell me all the gums when you were a little girl."

A few days later we walked to the corner store, and guess what we found? Bubble Yum and, tucked away in an odd corner, Hubba Bubba! On the way home Enzo was happy all over, skipping and gamboling along. "I can't believe they still have Hubba Bubba!" It was like when scientists catch a fish from great depths that was supposed to have been extinct for millions of years—a living fossil.

*

Enzo said, "When I get married, it's going to be a long road ahead."

"What does a long road ahead mean?"

"Weeks...and a day, I think."

"You mean a long road ahead *until* you get married?"

"Yeah. And then you can visit me when I go all the way to the farm."

*

Enzo and his friends are always telling each other their favorite this or that, and it gets very detailed. It's like they're all carving out these identities. I'm the kind of guy whose favorite ice cream is chocolate, and so on. So the other day I heard Enzo telling one of his friends that his *sixth* favorite color is orange.

47

May 9

Dear Max,

    Enzo: Sometimes I like girl things.

    Me: Like what?

    Enzo: Like big giant princess dresses. With princesses inside them. Jonathon doesn't like girl things. But I do. They remind me of superheroes.

May 14

Dear Max,

Enzo's playing with match box cars and some possible super hero type guy. I just asked him who the guy is, and he said, "He's ninja cat. He can transform, but ninjas can't really transform, but he's still a ninja."

Facts for the record:

Enzo learned to jump into the deep end of the pool on Saturday, and he jumped and jumped and jumped and jumped. He did the canon ball and the potato, which I invented because I can't do the canon ball. You just crouch by the edge of the pool in canon ball position, and then tip yourself in. Plop. He jumped in backwards and forwards. He went all the way to the bottom and shot back up.

We also like to pretend he's a dolphin and I'm his trainer. He has to jump over my floating body, or catch a pretend fish from my hand, or go through the underwater tunnel that I make with my legs. And we do underwater flips. Or I just throw him.

He has a shorty wetsuit, and already, in May, a wetsuit tan line so that when he's naked he looks like he's wearing a white wetsuit. His forearms and calves and shins and neck and hands are sweet, beautiful brown. We put sunscreen on him, really. He just turns brown in the light, instantly, like a chemical reaction, which I guess is what it is.

In the last month I've made very little money and gained seven pounds. Measures must be taken.

May 24

Dear Max,

At dinner Enzo asked Teresa, "Who was Martha Stewart's grandpa?"

"I don't know. Mr. Stewart I guess. How do you know who Martha Stewart is?"

"I just know."

*

When trying to convince us he's sick, he now looks sad and coughs and (this is the new part) clutches his heart. Then he adds, "Sometimes my heart feels bad."

*

Sometimes I watch him play when he's not noticing me and try to understand it. He'll have some dinosaurs, Scooby Doo characters, soldiers and super heroes all engaged in some world that's completely vivid to him and totally inscrutable to me.

His play is private and complete—the best thing in the world.

June 17

Dear Max,

Enzo's about to turn six. Sometimes it dawns on me, with panic, that any second now he won't be holding my hand to cross the street or jumping on my back from the couch, or snuggling my elbow, or calling me into his bedroom at least once every night.

He looks like such a grown up boy with his strong lively body. It seems like just a minute ago he had three rolls below the knee, and then we woke up one morning, and he had toned calves. And he does annoying six-year-oldish things like imitate this strange robotic voice that he learned from one of his least attractive friends.

He got nice little check marks in the right boxes on his Kindergarten report card, but the teacher added, "Enzo's over-use of his knowledge of animals is interfering with his kindergarten experience." Oh my. I asked Teresa if we should do something about that, talk to Mrs. Korte, start an anti-animal-fact campaign, and she said no. She's in the classroom one whole day a week, and she says he's doing fine. And if he likes animals, good.

He loves books about animals and brings them up in conversation out of the blue. Like he'll just walk up to a group and say, shyly, without eye contact, "Anacondas hunt Caymans. But Caymans aren't the anaconda's primary source of food." He needs to learn how to work the conversation around to his own pet subjects. And to look at people.

In Waldorf, five and six year olds are supposed to be in this world of physical play and make believe. That's why they don't do any letters or numbers. And mostly that's perfect for Enzo. They have a giant mud pit/dirt mountain in the playground. They go on long walks. They have their own simple cloth dolls called Wee Ones to take care of. At one of the parent workdays I started to weed an overgrown wild patch by the fence, and one of the kindergarten teachers rushed over to stop me because some of the kids had been making believe that fairies lived in the tall weeds.

Enzo's make-believe is never about fairies. It's about explosions. And he does adore facts.

June 29

Dear Max,

Enzo: Every boy has to have penis surgery. So they can get married.

*

Enzo to Teresa: How come you never drink wine?
Teresa: I've had wine before.
Enzo: I bet that was at the prom.
Teresa: The prom?
Enzo: That's an impossible thing. Wearing a pink dress.

*

Enzo (with an air of resignation): I think I'll just die now.

*

Enzo: I'm so strong I could lift this whole house with one butt-cheek.

*

Enzo: This is what a big kid looks like drinking soda. (Then he does this casual, slow walk, pretending to carry a drink in one hand.)

July 2

Dear Max,

On Enzo's sixth birthday we went out to pizza. He brought paper and colored pencils, and we played a game where Teresa would draw a picture and Enzo and I would try to guess what it was. So she drew two huge round circles next to each other, then some legs going down, knees, feet. Enzo watched, all attention, and finally shouted out, "Mama-Kate's butt!" Then Teresa drew quick little red lines coming out from between the butt cheeks. "Mama-Kate farting!" He laughed with delight, his eyes disappearing.

Then I drew two tiny circles next to each other, legs, knees. "It's an underwater scene," I said, and added little circles rising from the little circles. I don't draw, and everyone looked puzzled. "Enzo farting underwater!" I said. Again, delight, abandoned laughter, even a tiny scream of recognition.

Later Teresa and I were lying in bed and Enzo was asleep, "What are we going to do when he becomes too mature for us?" she said.

"I know. And it'll be in about thirty seconds." We lay quiet, a nice example of how present delight is always mixed with a little sadness because you know it will be gone soon. Even Enzo is big enough to feel this. He's always anticipating the future and trying to control it. "What are we doing tomorrow?" is his constant refrain. But I do think he can lose himself in delight better than we can.

Another example:
Enzo: Knock-Knock

Me: Who's there?
Enzo: Mama-Kate!
Me: Mama-Kate who?
Enzo: Mama-Kate in skinny jeans!

And as he's leading up the punch line his whole body and face are sparkling with anticipation. It's like Johnson rolling with joy at the thought that beamed in his eye.[1]

---

[1] Now that I've looked up the passage, the comparison seems less apt. But here it is. "An essay, written by Mr. Deane, a Divine of the Church of England, maintaining the future life of brutes, by an explication of certain parts of the scriptures, was mentioned, and the doctine insisted on by a gentleman who seemed found of curious speculation. Johnson, who did not like to hear of any thing concerning a future state which as not authorized by the regular canons of othodoxy, discouraged this talk; and being offended at its continuation, he watched an opportunity to give the gentlemean a blow of reprehansion. So, when the poor speculatist, with a serious metaphysical pensive face, addressed him, 'But really, Sir, when we see a very sensible dog, we don't know what to think of him,' Johnson, rolling with joy at the thought which beamed from his eye, turned quikly round, and replied, 'True, sir: and when we see a very foolish *fellow*, we don't know what to think of *him*.' He then rose up, strided to the fire, and stood for some time laughing and exulting." (*Life of Johnson*, Modern Library, 336, year 1768.)

July 10

Dear Max,

>Enzo: Guess what I want for Christmas?
>Me: How could I possibly guess?
>Enzo: Besides a remote control rattle snake.
>Me: I don't know.
>Enzo: Jewels.

*

Yesterday I was putting sunscreen on Enzo, and he was being a pain in the ass about it. He said, "I'm never going to wear sunscreen again. I'm going to throw it in the trash."

"I'm going to the bathroom now. If I come back and the sunscreen is in the trash, I'm going to give you a time out. Mama-Teresa isn't the only one who can do that you know." I peed and came back. The sunscreen was not in the trash. He was standing next to it, looking fierce and proud. "Thanks, honey, you did the right thing."

"Only Mama-Teresa can make me cry."

July 12

Dear Max,

I'm in a strange state of mind. I hope I can write about it.

I'm editing my diary from 1994 and just got through all the battles I fought in grad school to be able to write about Boswell and Johnson the way I wanted to. And then I got to the part about reading *The Rainbow* and also re-reading a paper that Annie wrote about *The Rainbow*—as an example of perfect criticism—so much in the spirit of the book that you feel as if you've just read the book but with a borrowed and more powerful attention. The paper is very long, and it was published in *Spectrum*, so I had a copy, and I typed the whole thing into my diary. You have to have just read *The Rainbow* to understand it, and so I think I've decided not to include it in my edited diary. But just reading it made tears come into my eyes. Everything lovable about Lawrence and about Annie seemed to be right there.

Then I started thinking about this lawyer friend, a man, about sixty, and how he loves Johnson too, which I just happened to find out somehow when we were driving back downtown from the branch jail. Months later we talked about Johnson again, and he started saying bad things about Boswell—he was a drunk and a leech and a letcher. And just now I was fantasizing about saying to Bill that if he really didn't love Boswell I would have to break up with him as my imaginary boyfriend. And if you love Johnson you should kiss the ground that Boswell walked on. Bill is a lovely guy, and not just because he loves Johnson. (He's not really my imaginary boyfriend—he's too old, fat and golf-crazy for that—but I do like him.) In trial he makes all the right arguments, he's effective and committed and really good. And there always seems to be this part of him hovering above it all, completely amused.

But what I wanted to write about was that I was fantasizing all over again about telling him I would have to break up with him. In the fantasy we were in an elevator (*why?*) and Noah Phillips, a DA that I know and like, was there too (*why?*), and I was telling Bill how wrong he was about Boswell, and the whole time I was having this fantasy, I was sitting in this big brown chair, comfortably reclined with my laptop on my lap and tears running down my face.

July 13

Dear Max,

Enzo just woke up and immediately got a bloody nose. Not from injury but just spontaneously. (We're in Tahoe, so maybe it's the dry air and altitude.)

"Mom! I got a bloody nose!"

I rushed over and put a paper towel to his nose, but it had already stopped bleeding. But there was blood on his shirt, both hands, arms, legs, the couch. "I have six meters of blood and after that I'll be dead, " he said.

July 16

Dear Max,

    I'm home alone. Enzo and Teresa are still in Lake Tahoe. It's strange, and lonely and wonderful and then lonely again.

July 24

Dear Max,

Enzo jumped off the diving board yesterday. He looked so small walking slowly to the end of the board.

He'd been thinking about it for a while. Several times he said, "Mama-Kate, if you go off, I'll go off." I said I'd already jumped off and I was all dry so I wasn't going off again. But I walked with him over to the deep end and stood with him and watched the big kids jump.

"You don't have to do it if you don't want to."

"I know that."

And then instead he just jumped into the pool from the side for a while and then went back to the shallow end. But he kept walking back to the diving board and looking. And then he walked up the little stairs and slowly to the end of the board and just jumped. I expected him to peer down for a while and maybe just walk back. But there was no pause.

Then he did it again and again and again, finally running at full speed down the length of the board and launching himself off the end.

July 29

Dear Max,

Today is my birthday. I love my birthday. And guess what? I am thin! (For me. And for this diary of record, that means 146 pounds.)

Enzo and Teresa got me a small bottle of Beano To Go, a lavender scarf with a subtle snakeskin pattern and a hat. Hurrah!

*

I was just putting away my clothes. My closet is in Enzo's bedroom. He was on his bed with some cars, driving them around and making revving noises. Teresa walked by and said something, and I replied. Ordinary talk.

"Can you guys give me some peace and quiet!" Enzo said.

*

Yesterday Enzo asked me if I have seen a clown in real life and asked what clowns really look like. I tried to describe. Then he said, "Clowns are a symbol of god."

"I'm not so sure about that."

"I've known that since I was a baby. Keelan told me that."

His life is so mysterious.

August 14

Dear Max,

Teresa and Enzo are home again. It's just like sunshine flooding in.

I don't think I explained that we all went up to Tahoe, and Teresa and Enzo decided to stay. Guess they read the weather report, which was triple digits in Sacramento with no end in sight. And I was going to have to work long hours and weekends to make up for the time off. And we were planning to return the next weekend anyway for Teresa's birthday. So they stayed and I took the bus home.

I was alone for four days. It was strange and luxurious and then strange again. And when Teresa texted that they were coming home early, I texted back, just come today, come now. So they did.

While they were gone, Teresa told me that Enzo said, "You're is just as much fun as mama-Kate." Ha! She also told me that when there was thunder in the distance he said, "That's mama-Kate!" It's nice to know he didn't forget about me entirely. So they were fine, and I was fine, but after four days Teresa wanted to come home and bribed him with extra TV so that he agreed. I don't think he missed me. He was having fun and he had Teresa. I guess I'm glad he didn't.

Even after four days Enzo is different. He looks older than I remembered. His hair seems messy in a new way, and he has new expressions, probably picked up from his new *Scooby-Doo* video.

It's funny how attracted he is to cliché phrases and how fresh they sound coming from him. I can't remember exactly what it was, but something like, *on the edge of my seat* or *within an inch of my life*. I'll listen today and get it right. When he takes up a new phrase he tends to apply it in all sorts of situations.

August 16

Dear Max,

So I took some notes on Enzo's expressions:

To me: Caught you red-handed with your evil fart schemes!"

To himself: (peering at his Star Wars figures) There's one guy missing that I cannot put my finger on...oh there he is.

August 18

Dear Max,

A few nights ago Enzo woke up in the middle of the night and called for me. I sat on his bed and he snuggled around my butt. After a few minutes I quietly got up, hoping he was asleep. "That was amazing, mom," he said and then went back to sleep.

Today is Teresa's birthday. Enzo is sick.

August 27

Dear Max,

Enzo says he wants to be home schooled.

God forbid.

He read about it in a book. That is, we read him a book about different kinds of families and different things that people do and how it's all okay and no one should ever feel bad about anything, and now he knows about home schooling and wants it.

I asked him what he would do in home school.

"I don't know. Draw a lot. Make robots. Out of recycled objects. I could make hearts out of paper."

That actually sounds about right.

September 1

Dear Max,

"Snow cones are my main source of diet," Enzo informs me.

September 3

Dear Max,

      Enzo: I killed a spider.
      Me: Why?
      Enzo: I was suffering from arachnophobia.

*

      He claims he's allergic to water. I can't remember if I was trying to get him to bathe or drink.

*

      We went fishing yesterday and the day before. And I will just whisper in your private ear, Max—*fuck fishing.*

September 5

Dear Max,

I'm applying for state jobs. I don't want any of them, but we need the money and dental work looms. But what is the difference between The Department of Managed Care and The Department of Health Care Services and the Managed Risk Medical Insurance Board?

The one job I can imagine doing is Administrative Law Judge, or ALJ. I imagine myself being very kind and fair in these sober, chic outfits, and not working very hard. I told Teresa about the ALJ job, and she looked puzzled. "Justice League of America? Are you actually Wonder Woman?"

Enzo just woke up and immediately brushed his teeth and washed his face. He came out of the bathroom and showed me his teeth. I said they were sparkling. I asked him why he's into washing and brushing these days.

"I have to look good," he said.

"Why? You always look good."

"So the kids in my class will like me."

He started school yesterday, and I'm happy to say he is very well liked. Thank god.

September 7

Dear Max,

Enzo: Did you fart in college?
Me: Yeah.
Enzo: Is that where you learned to fart more than a lot?

*

Teresa asked Enzo to do something, probably take a bath or pick up toys, and he said, "Naw...not ma thing."

*

Keelan came over for dinner last night. He asked Enzo, "Do you know all the planets?"
"Not officially," said Enzo.

*

I'm listening to this audio book about personal productivity. It's about how you should discipline yourself to do the worst biggest most important job first and keep doing it until it's done and then you will feel really good about yourself and so will everybody else and you will make more money and get promoted. It has chapters like, "Focus on Key Result Areas" and "Leverage Your Special Talents."

I only listen to it at work during lunchtime when I take my nap, and I find it so restful and satisfying to lie on the red velvet couch in my office listening to such tips as, "Motivate Yourself Into Action" and then I never learn how because I am asleep.

It fills me with this delicious sense of comfort that I will never, never be like that.

*

I just remembered to write that when Enzo grows up he wants to work in a submarine and be a farmer on the weekends.

September 11

Dear Max,

Enzo started school again, and I've been pumping him for information about the new kids. He's not very forthcoming, but he did say that he threw cat poop at Magnus and then Magnus threw sand and cat poop at him and got it in his eye.

"Well, it sounds like you started it. Did anyone tell Mrs. Korte that there's cat poop in the sandbox?"

"No. We made a dumpster and put the cat poop in the dumpster. It was called the cat poop dumpster."

"How did you make it?"

"Out of sand. Everybody helped. We're keeping it a secret. Mrs.Korte says there are no secrets in our class, but there are."

*

We read *Charlie and the Chocolate Factory* to Enzo, and he loved it. Luckily, I can dial down my reading comprehension to zero and just think about other stuff, but I did pay a little attention, and my god it's an awful book. I did love the fact that he loved it though. One of the best things about being a kid is reading and reading with pure forgetfulness—no taste, all appetite.

As soon as he can do that by himself, everything will be perfect.

*

You know how I'm applying for State Jobs? I got an email from the personnel department of the DMV asking for two writing samples. I guess that means I made the first cut. And if I get the job, all I have to do is fake my own death. But first, I would get some dental work done.

September 14

Dear Max,

    I was explaining community property to Teresa. We aren't getting divorced. A couple on *The L Word* are. They have money and lawyers. I said we wouldn't need that—we'd be easy because everything we have is community property, and you just split it down the middle. Teresa thought about that for a moment. "I don't want half of what we have. I want half of better stuff."

*

    Enzo still has that picture of Kyriana in his room. Teresa heard him explaining to Keelan that she's his girlfriend.
    "Where does she live?" said Keelan.
    "Lake Tahoe."
    "Do you ever see her?"
    "I try to."
    Later Enzo said to me, "I know she has her cast off by now. But maybe she has another cast."
    "Why do you like casts so much?"
    "I'm not going to tell you. It's a secret."

*

    Enzo to me: Can I take a picture of your butt?
    And later: Your butt is the biggest ever reported.

September 15

Dear Max,

Enzo woke up and said he wanted to read *Encyclopedia Brown*. By himself. "I want to read it in privacy."

Yes!

But I do feel a tiny bit left out.

I need to spy on him and see what exactly this reading is. He can't *read* read. *Encyclopedia Brown* only has a few pictures for each story. So is he just staring at the words? Looking at the pictures and remembering the stories?

*

Now he's watching TV and eating buttered white toast and frozen mango chunks. He's sick, and he gets treats when he's sick, like white bread and frozen treats. But he just told me that he doesn't want any more butter. "I can't *see* when I eat butter."

Another mystery.

*

I have an interview at the Department of Health Care Services on Thursday. I wonder what they do there.

September 22

Dear Max,

I was stepping up to the bed and then down again, over and over, holding my hand weights and puffing away, while the bed creaked and sagged and Duncan looked at me with mild annoyance—but not enough annoyance to move off the bed. Teresa walked by, looking amused. "You shouldn't laugh! Do you have any idea how fat I could be? You know how fat I was in college?" She didn't know me then, but she's seen pictures. "Just imagine me that fat and then add five pounds a year for twenty years. That's three hundred and seventy pounds."

"How yeah?" she said, "Well you have no idea what a drunk I could be. You think I'm an asshole now?"

She went on with whatever she was doing. A few minutes later she passed by again. I was still puffing away. "Too mature to say anything," she said as she glided by.

*

Enzo: Boobs! Armpits!
Teresa: Cracks! Crotches!

*

Enzo: When I grow up I'm going to have two jobs. Gold mining and rock star. Actually four jobs. Check! Submarine. Farmer. Gold mining. Rock Star.

*

For the record, and this is terrifying, but also okay I think, I had a job interview at the Department of Health Care Services, and I think it went pretty well. I liked the people, and I always think that people I like are going to like me back. Sometimes that turns out not to be true, and it's shocking. They do Medi Cal. Lord have mercy.

September 24

Dear Max,

Enzo and I camped out in the back yard. Enzo had five tiny boxes of gum from the Japanese grocery store. "I'm going to combine all my gums to make one powerful gum."

"How much gum do you have in your mouth right now?"

"Millions."

For the backyard camping trip, Enzo got out binoculars, a hand-held microscope, several flashlights and miscellaneous other toys and possessions. "We're going to look for critters, bats, owls...night stuff."

As we were lying in our sleeping bags in the dark, he said, "Do you know one of the best days of my life?"

"What?"

"I hate to say it. Disneyland."

October 10

Dear Max,

Enzo said, "Girls look better than boys."

"Why?"

"They just do. But boys make better rock stars."

I was thinking about that and about little boy brains and how strange they are and wondering what it will be like when that strange boy mind gets dosed with testosterone, dear god. I wondered if boys need that to become their smartest selves, their whole selves. (Yes, of course they do.)

Girls are so together at Enzo's age. Some of them seem almost like little grownups (and I don't mean the ones dressed in slut clothes). Boys are just savage wild beasts, and, frankly, not that bright.

Of course Enzo's a genius in his own winning way, but he does have some strange ideas. And if you ever try to play rock-paper-scissors with him he usually chooses gun.

*

Enzo says I have two mangos in my boobs, and two coconuts in my butt and a watermelon in my tummy. It all sounds like some kind of Polynesian fertility goddess, and I do take issue with the watermelon, but still I love it that he pays attention to me. He ignores us a lot now, shutting his door firmly, sealing off his universe. We knock before entering.

Teresa found out that one of Enzo's kindergarten classmates has *almost* the same sperm donor as Enzo. We tried for several months with this one donor, half German, half black, a gardener, but I never got pregnant, so we switched to someone else for good luck. Well, Enzo's classmate's donor is from the same sperm bank, half German, half black and a gardener. It has to be the same guy. So she's his almost-accidental-half-sister.

Last night Teresa and I were lying in bed trying to picture Enzo with black people's hair

*

Enzo: You're lucky to have a boy that shoots ice out of his butt. And every other part. And makes an ice slide.

October 21

Dear Max,

    Enzo: Mom, are you thinking what I'm thinking?
    Me: I don't know.
    Enzo: I'm thinking we should dress Duncan up as a baby jaguar.

*

    Enzo: Your butt smells like quesadillas.
    Me: It does not. It smells like beautiful flowers.
    Enzo: It smells like quesadillas.
    (This is our punishment for teaching him the expression "cut the cheese." He's just taking it to its logical conclusion.)

*

    Enzo: Did you know that boogers are part of our survival?

*

    Enzo: (Naming candy bars to be made in his factory.) *Spider Web Colossal, Goldfish Snap Jacks, Blood Barrel.*
    Charlie and the Chocolate Factory probably brought that on. By the way, it's a horrible book. He loved it, of course. Because he has no taste.

I have to issue a correction. I wrote earlier that Enzo said I have two mangos in my boobs, and two coconuts in my butt and a watermelon in my tummy. Actually, it was two watermelons in my butt and a coconut in my tummy. Mangos the same.

I'm trying to figure out if this is an improvement.

October 26

Dear Max,

Enzo gave me a pomelo from the back yard with two eyes made of seeds stuck into the rind and two red tacks stuck in the top where the stem used to be.

"Thank you! Did you make that?"

"Yes."

"I love it!"

"Would you like to get me a gift too?"

"I was thinking I would make you a homemade thank you card."

"I think a Target-made gift would do."

The pomelo sat on the kitchen counter for a few days, and then I threw it away. That night Enzo was doing experiments in the kitchen, and when he was throwing something away, he saw the pomelo in the trash.

"You threw away my gift."

"I'm sorry, honey. It was starting to go bad. You know how we have to throw away our Halloween pumpkins after a while? It's like that."

I dug the pomelo out of the trash, rinsed it off and put it in the fridge. I told Enzo we could get cloves and stick them in the pomelo, just like when Laura made a clove apple in *Little House in the Big Woods*, and then it would smell good and never go bad.

Do we really have to do this now? Fuck.

A couple of times Enzo has asked me if we can adopt another kid. One time he said, "I think we should adopt a really beautiful girl. But that would cost twice as much." And then he added, "Sometimes people ask me if I'm adopted." Something about his tone made me think he liked the idea.

He looks pretty different from both of us, and I've had people ask me where we adopted him from. But one of the kindergarten teachers (not his but the next classroom over) came up to me and said, "You must be Enzo's other mom. He looks just like you." And I went into a glow. We both have tiny Asian eyes, but they look better on him because he's half Chinese.

October 29

Dear Max,

I took a shower while Enzo took a bath. (The shower is a separate stall.) We got out at the same time. Enzo slapped my wet butt with a resounding smack. "I love spanking your butt, mom. It gives me joy. So much joy."

I felt like saying, "Me too!" but instead I said something like, "Go get your pajamas on, you turkey."

I ran and wrote down what he said right away, but the pad of paper is in his room and he's asleep, so I can't check it right now. As Boswell said, nothing remains the same when put in different words. But I'll check it later.

I don't want to give you the impression that he's allowed to just haul off and hit us. It's just that he and my butt have a special relationship. We play this game where I back up to him shaking my butt, trying to corner him and squash him like a little bug, and he defends himself with self-styled karate moves. Perhaps I should add that the game is normally played clothed.

October 30

Dear Max,

Last Sunday Enzo and I were at the park playing *Little House In the Big Woods*. This means he pretends to be Pa and shoot and skin animals while I lie in a big plastic tube that's part of the play structure and pretend to lie in wait with my gun. I like it because I don't have to do anything but lie there. After a while he said, "Let's go to town and trade our furs and get some nachos."

He has never had nachos. Not that we have anything against them. We just haven't gotten around to them with him.

I told him about the Nacho Debacho—the time that Teresa and I made nachos with everything on them and ate them all, an overeating event so epic that it came to have a name.

October 31

Dear Max,

Last night I dreamed that the judge in the trial I'm in was sentencing Enzo to life in prison without the possibility of parole. It looks funny as I write it, but it was terrible in the dream. I was yelling, "He's only six! And he was only *five* when all this happened!" I don't know what he'd done, but something serious. The judge said that he would get the treatment that he needs in prison.

When I woke up it made me think of Pricilla Shorter, our client's mom, showing up with nice clothes for him to wear to court, patient, worried, sick with cancer herself, wearing flip-flops with toe socks because of some foot infection. Jesus Christ.

Shannon will get life without parole if convicted, and there's nothing the judge can do about it. The last trial, the jury hung 11 to 1 for guilt. The charges are robbery, kidnapping, torture, murder and arson.

It's not as bad as it sounds. It's a robbery gone wrong. Sometimes these things spin out of control. There are two co-defendants and probably some uncharged participants as well.

November 2

Dear Max,

Last night I played *Hiss* with Enzo. It's sort of like dominos but you play in with colored snake segments. I resisted the temptation to let him win. When he saw that I was going to win he tried to explain a new rule that would make him win. I still resisted. Finally he conceded. He said, "You can't tell but I'm totally crying in my heart."

November 3

Dear Max,

Last night at dinner it was just me and Enzo, because Teresa was out in her studio. Enzo said, "I want to pray. Do you know any prayers?"

"Sure. You hold hands like this. *Bless oh Lord this food to our use and us to thy service and make us ever mindful of the needs of others.* And then you say *Amen.*"

"That makes, like, *no* sense."

"Do you want to make a prayer?"

"Yeah." He folded his hands and closed his eyes. (Where did he learn this?) "Thank you Jesus for this house and for keeping bad robbers out of this house."

"Amen."

"Amen."

"What made you think about Jesus?"

"He's our god."

"Okay."

"There's also a god with a bow and arrow. That's the god of love."

"Cupid?"

"Yeah. I want to do another one. Jesus please send us some salmon. Thank you. Amen."

And then we ate our salmon.

November 11

Dear Max,

Enzo told me that Jesus and an Angel got together and made Santa Claus. "An angel is a girl, right?"

He knows all about eggs and sperm, so at least his sex education is going well. As for his religious instruction—oh dear. For example, an angel is not a girl—at least not the really famous ones that even I know about. I didn't think to tell him any of this at the time. I just said, "Um, I'm not sure," and looked noncommittal.

I'm thinking about dragging him to church during Advent. That way we won't feel like such assholes when we show up on Christmas Eve. We used to go to church now and then, and then less and less and now we're pretty much Sunday school dropouts.

Have I mentioned that I'm an atheist? But I'm afraid that Enzo might end up being one of those people with religious feeling, and if he knows nothing about the religion of his ancestors, who knows what direction he'll take it?

Better a Lutheran than a Moonie.

He also asked me if Santa Claus steals.

"No!" I said.

"Then how does he get all those toys?"

"Haven't you ever heard of Santa's workshop?"

I think he bought it.

*

Enzo: Mom, can you make me mad?

Me: Okay. (Thinking for a minute.) Go to your room right now! And don't come out!"

Enzo: No. You have to hit me.

Me: Okay. (I pretend-hit him.)

Enzo: Harder! You have to hit me hard. That's the only thing to bring out my powers."

(I try a few more times, and he eventually gives up on me. No powers. He wanders off and into his own play.)

November 12

Dear Max,

Last night I was snuggling Enzo in bed. He rubbed his eyes and yawned in classic sleepy fashion. "That means you're really tired," I said.

"I'm at my weakest at night," he said.

"Yeah."

"If you ever want to kill me, you can do it at night."

"But why would I want to kill you?"

"If you were starving."

"I'd kill mama Teresa."

"Or you could make a coat out of my back fat. And sell it for a few dollars."

"I don't think so."

"Or sell my jaws as a collectible."

The killing and maiming part doesn't really bother me, but when did he become so grasping? Like when we ripped out the old mostly dead green bean plants from the garden, he carefully saved the hardened yellow pods. "I'm going to sell them for a dollar each."

November 22

Dear Max,

I dreamed that I started my new job. The dream was filled with dread. It was set in a big unfamiliar European-feeling city. The dread had to do with being late and not being able to find the office. Also with the fact that once I got there, one of my duties would involve babysitting.

November 24

Dear Max,

Shannon Shorter got convicted, after a week of deliberations, of murder in the course of a robbery, and now he'll serve life in prison without the possibility of parole. The two co-defendants got convicted too. I wasn't there for the verdict, and my role in the trial was small. But I've known him for almost three years, and I like him, and he says he's innocent. God I hope that's not true. But it sure seems true when you're with him.

I was at the beach in Santa Barbara when I picked up a message from the department 12 clerk that verdicts were in. By the time I picked up the message, it was several hours old. I texted the lead attorney, "What happened?" and he texted back "All guilty of 187 and 211 special."

It was one of those beautiful fall days, clear and warm and a little windy. Surfers kept trotting by, hurried and eager, not wanting to miss one minute in the water. Enzo learned to boogie board. We had great sandwiches. Shannon only came into my mind a few times.

When I did my first DUI trial ten years ago, I couldn't believe that my obviously guilty client could be convicted, and when he was, I was devastated.

You get used to things. That's probably mostly a bad thing. But you have to survive.

I even felt a tiny twinge of relief. It's over. Another hung jury would have meant another trial. Twice is enough.

November 26

Dear Max,

Five thirty of the morning I start my new job. I'm trying to think of the whole thing as one prolonged excuse to shop, but I just remembered that I don't really like shopping anymore.

Please let my office have a window.

I got a packet in the mail that included a summary of benefits (goody!) and a ten page organizational chart for the department of social services. The department has ten divisions. The legal division is one. I'm in the enforcement section of the legal division. The chart for each division is like a giant family tree. Looking it all over, it seemed so unlikely that any of it would work, but I know that it does, somehow.

I'm trying to remember Wallace Stevens and Kafka. Didn't they work for insurance companies? And then there's Trollope and his beloved Post Office.

Just to prove I'm not dead, I'm going to write about it. There! It's an assignment. I'm going to be a good reporter. The worse the job is, the more fun it will be to write about it.

By the way, I'm sitting in my newly set up office at home. I haven't had my own desk at home in about five years. I've just migrated from couch to bed to chair, clutching my laptop and trying not to lose my writing entirely. Maybe with my very own place to write, I will. But for right now, can I please read?

I went to see Shannon Shorter. He sat down. He was smiling, half-laughing, and his arms were trembling. Maybe his whole body was trembling but you could see it in his arms.

"I'm sorry," I said.

"That's all right."

I asked him if he was eating or sleeping. Eating a little. No sleep. I asked him if it's different in here now that he's been convicted. "No one says anything. But they don't want to look me in the eye. It's like they're scared of me now. It's like they're scared because if I can get convicted then something's not right. They know I didn't do it."

I asked him the details of the verdicts. He said he was found not guilty of the kidnap, the torture, and the arson. Guilty of the robbery and the murder. It's a puzzling verdict. I thought it was an all-or-nothing case.

He asked me what he should do when he gets to prison. Would he have to join a gang? I said I didn't know, but I hoped not. I'm pretty ashamed of how little I know about prison. He smiled and shrugged and said, "Guess I'll have to act like a tough guy now. And I was always just into the girls. I'll be all right."

He thanked me for coming and said he considered me a friend. He asked me to come see him one more time before he gets sentenced.

Life in prison. His whole life. Guaranteed to die there.

Even if he is guilty, it doesn't seem right.

November 29

Dear Max,

Shannon's mom called me. She said, "I feel the way I felt when I first got cancer. I just feel like I need to apologize for everything. I've cried all I can. And now I need to do something."

There's nothing she can do, but I didn't say that. I explained how appeals work.

In the background Shannon's little daughter wanted to be lifted up to wash her hands. "I can't lift you up," said Pricilla, "You know my arm's not working right. Here, you just use the hand cleaner." And then to me, "My right side goes out sometimes, and it's hard for her to understand."

December 8

Dear Max,

Disneyland with Enzo, where I learned that it's possible to be terrified, nauseated, bored and happy, all at the same time. A nice compressed example the mixedness of experience. Enzo's hopes were so high that I thought surely he'd be disappointed. He wasn't.

December 10

Dear Max,

    Fuck.

    Last night I bought a dishwasher off Craigslist and got ripped off, and I feel so foolish! I keep thinking about how good I felt driving away, how happy that I didn't just buy a dishwasher at Sears but instead met these nice people and got such a good deal on a top of the line dishwasher that I'm now pretty sure is an empty shell.

    Sarah, the woman who sold it to me, said that when she was a little girl she used to fantasize that her name was Kate. I told her that my sister's name was Sarah. We bonded. Two strong men loaded the dishwasher while we held the hoses and made helpful remarks.

    The dishwasher was advertised at $175, and I had talked her down—thinking I was so Craigslist savvy—to $150. After the dishwasher was loaded, I gave her $160, and she want to get my change. It was dark. She was gone for a moment, then back and said, "You only gave me $110." I apologized, embarrassed, and gave her two nice fresh twenty dollar bills. So I think I actually paid $180 for a dishwasher that almost certainly doesn't work. I mean, if you're going to scam, why not go all the way?

    Should I call the police?

    But what if the dishwasher does work but I don't get to keep it because it turns out to be stolen property? Besides, the cops will probably just smile. It's so small time. And it was nice of the scammers not to rob and murder me. Perhaps I'll let it go.

December 12

Dear Max,

   I have to report that I didn't get ripped off after all. Teresa found the missing forty bucks on the floor of the car. Faith in humanity restored. Faith in self diminished. How ready I was to believe the worst!

December 15

Dear Max,

My dad's birthday. He turns seventy today, I think. Long live daddy! (Actually sixty-nine, I found out later.)

He doesn't seem old. He has work that he likes, and he works hard. He's in the world. He's cheerful, if a bit predictable.

I hope I remember to call him.

*

Enzo: Cowboy's never pass their driving test.
Me: Really?
Enzo: They just go wild when they drive. Like they're in the desert, riding a real horse.

*

Enzo: Do you know what a wedgie means?
Me: Yeah. Do you?
Enzo: Yeah.
Me: What does it mean?
Enzo: No. *You* say.
Me: It means...(trailing off...pretending to think).
Enzo: It means a kiss.

December 24

Dear Max,

I told Enzo that we're going to church on Christmas Eve to learn what Christmas is all about. "It's Jesus's birthday. If it weren't for his birthday, there wouldn't be any Christmas."

"I don't want to celebrate Jesus's birthday. I want to celebrate Santa's Merry Christmas."

I don't care about Jesus's birthday either, but I like the Christmas carols and the candles and the people.

We'll probably just go to Target.

*

Enzo: If I were a girl I would *not* want to be a shepherd girl in the Himalayas. The Yeti—to legend—the Yeti eats mostly shepherd girls.

December 29

Dear Max,

Almost New Year's Resolution time. Goody!

I just checked the beginning of this year's diary to see if there were any resolutions that should be recycled, and there weren't any resolutions at all. What was I thinking? No wonder I spent the entire year getting fatter and dumber.

Possible resolutions: eat oatmeal, read *The Iliad*, promote my books in some later-to-be-defined way, start food blog again, wear color, brush hair, discipline son.

Made in the USA
San Bernardino, CA
30 October 2013